Acknowledgements

Windy Old Fossils would not have been possible without the encouragement, belief and vision of Elizabeth Freestone and the Pentabus team both past and present. Also, Simon Longman for his patience and good humour, alongside actors Joanna Bacon and Ian Barritt who brought Ted and Lizzie to life, as well as the expert production team. Special thanks to my agent Nick Quinn and everyone at The Agency for their constant support; Steph Morris for proofreading and Ronaldo Alves for the wonderful cover. Finally, huge thanks to my publisher Nadia Kingsley at Fair Acre Press who has truly made this book possible.

I0234040

Fair Acre Press

First published in Great Britain in 2019 by Fair Acre Press
www.fairacrepress.co.uk

A CIP catalogue record for this book is available from the British Library

ISBN 978-1-911048-37-4

Typeset by Nadia Kingsley

Cover Design by Ronaldo Alves

Back Cover photographs: © Robert Workman
from *Windy Old Fossils*, Pentabus 2014 with actors Joanna Bacon and Ian Barritt.

Windy Old Fossils

was first produced by

Pentabus

as part of

The Young Writers' Festival 2014 at

The Charlton Arms, Ludlow

1st – 5th July 2014

Lizzie	Joanna Bacon
Ted	Ian Barritt

Director Elizabeth Freestone

Designer Neil Irish

Lighting Designer Elanor Higgins

Sound Designer Fergus O'Hare

For Elizabeth

PENTABUS
RURAL THEATRE COMPANY

www.pentabus.co.uk

INTRODUCTION

When I think about this play I think about a landscape so open that it feels like the fields, hills and trees are more a wide ocean than land. And these two people are lost within that.

Their little house, like a life raft floating in a sea of green and brown.

A raft that's unfairly falling to pieces.

And Lizzie and Ted cling on, as they drift through memory and isolation with humour and sadness.

It's a play about the countryside and being forgotten within that landscape.

And we need stories like this to remind us all how easily that can happen. And how unfair it is.

Simon Longman

It was a crazy idea, in retrospect.
To produce eight brand new plays by eight brand new writers.
In a pop-up theatre.
In two weeks.

But, like many crazy ideas, it somehow worked.

Stories were told, audiences were moved and writers – well, writers were happy. Which was the whole point.

We'd launched a Young Writers Programme the previous autumn. I'd been determined to offer young people living in the countryside a way to express themselves about things that mattered to them. And, if they wanted, to use the experience to pursue a creative career – although that was by no means the endgame. Just being heard, having the chance to develop writing skills and to find your voice; that was the point. In that autumn, eight young playwrights came to Pentabus. They met regularly, took part in workshops, met professional theatre makers, experimented with ideas and learnt their craft. As the group wrote more and more I began to be, firstly, impressed and inspired by their imaginations, and, secondly, convinced that seeing their work produced was the most useful next step we could offer them. And so the idea of the Young Writers Festival was born.

The logistics were epic. Eight plays. Eight writers. Several drafts of each play, all of which needed to **be** read, noted, responded to, rewritten and read again. Four directors directing two plays each. Three designers creating the sets, costume, lights and sound for each play. Ten actors performing in two or three (or even four) plays each. Three rehearsal spaces operating all day every day.

From finding a performance space to raising the money; from working out the cross-casting (which actor would be in which play) to building the sets; from scheduling rehearsals to selling tickets, the Pentabus team – Executive Director Rachael Griffin, Producer Verity Overs-Morrell, Finance Officer Lynda Lynne, Stage Manager Sam Eccles, Technical Assistant Ollie Farr, Marketing Officer Crayg Ward, and our writer-in-residence Simon Longman who took on the mantle of Festival Curator – exhausted and excelled themselves.

Being in rehearsals was thrilling. Knowing that in other spaces around the farm (where Pentabus is based) other writers, directors, and actors were working on brand new plays, just like we were, made for a feverishly creative atmosphere. I directed two plays in the Festival, a wonderful ghost story by Michael Wild called *Sea Breeze*.
And Tom Wentworth's *Windy Old Fossils*.
I knew right away it was a cracker. Even from rough

early drafts, it was clear Tom had something to say and a style in which to say it. There aren't many plays about older people, and none that I can think of about older people struggling to make ends meet in the countryside. Even more surprising is that as a young man Tom wrote with such understanding and compassion about these characters. It was a story that mattered – to him, to the world and, I had no doubt, to the audience. Fuel poverty is a very real and dangerously secret part of many older people's experience. Tom had found a way to explore this subject with wit and humanity. Simon and I nudged him through a few drafts, with suggestions about story and structure. The language and voices of the characters he had found early on. Ted and Lizzie have a unique relationship (beautifully played in our production by Ian Barritt and Joanna Bacon). Squabbling and loving siblings, they both have sadness in their pasts and fears for their future. Their dialogue encompasses high comedy alongside painful emotional truths. They work to keep each other's spirits up, fight like cat and dog when the other does something they don't like, and ultimately comfort each other in the (literally) dark nights of the soul. They are a terrific couple of parts for any actor.

That's not to say the play doesn't present its challenges – scenes taking place in the dark; an off-stage wind turbine, bits of which need to find their way onstage at various points; not to mention a working exercise bike that 'powers' the electricity. Our creative team did a terrific job with excellently sourced props, clever lighting and a super sound world complete with all kinds of weather and turbine clanks. Together they conjured up all that we needed the audience to see on stage, and all that we needed them to imagine off it.

Tom's a generous writer. In *Windy Old Fossils* he gives the actors lines they can wring every drop of comedy and tragedy from. He gives the creative team images and suggestions that can be interpreted literally or theatrically, as they wish. And he gives the audience an intriguing and accessible story that delivers what it promises, and so much more. I couldn't be more pleased that the text is being published and hope it leads to many more productions of the play. Not least because I want to see how other people problem-solve the wind turbine!

Elizabeth Freestone
Director

THE SCRIPT

CHARACTERS

Lizzie Kirkpatrick, 73

Ted Stevens, 75

The action takes place in a dilapidated cottage in the wilds of Shropshire in 2014.

/ indicates where a speaker is interrupted by another person

Note: Each projection of the turbine should be accompanied by an appropriate sound giving a sense each time of the outside world creeping ever closer in.

The distant echoing of a clanking, rusty old wind turbine. Its shadow on the wall, moving. A quarter turn... Then –

Silence.

ONE

Autumn.

The living room of Ted and Lizzie's cottage is in blackness. It's an old room with peeling paper and shelving stuffed full of records on one side and two comfortable armchairs in the middle. It is obviously being lived in and a two-ring burner has been situated near to the chairs, whilst an exercise bike is near the door. LIZZIE's knitting is under her chair. Photos of LIZZIE's husband Alan are dotted around. A door offstage leads to the kitchen and outside and at the back of the room there is a brazier.

There's been a power cut and LIZZIE and TED are on their hands and knees, in pyjamas (with layers on top and underneath), searching for something at opposite ends of the room. When they do get up they both look fairly tall and upright. At this point in time they are still quite physically active.

Lizzie Ted Stevens I could murder you sometimes. Really I could!

Ted I've said I'm sorry! It was an accident.

Lizzie What was the final thing I said to you last

night?

Ted   Change the batteries in the torch.

Lizzie   Exactly.

Ted   But they were dead and there's none left. I looked everywhere. Lizzie, please don't be angry.

Lizzie   It's not that Ted. You never think ahead.

Ted   I'm sorry but...

Lizzie   Did you think to take a candle to bed with you, just in case? No.

Ted   I came downstairs for a candle this morning though.

Lizzie   Then lost it.

Ted   You made me jump creeping up behind me like that.

Lizzie   You could have been a burglar!

Ted   No-one would burgle this place.

Lizzie   There could be a Shropshire crime wave.

Ted   Out here? Even the postman doesn't come here anymore.

Lizzie No. I'll have you know I have some items of great value, there's Alan's collection for a start...

Ted I mean no-one would ever come all this way. Especially for your late husband's jazz standards.

Lizzie I'll have you know some of them are collectables. *(Of candle)* Where can it be? We need that candle Ted.

Ted We'll find it, don't you worry, Lizzie.

Lizzie Perhaps if we work our way towards each other instead of just... I can't believe this.

Ted Right. I can't really see you. Wave!

Lizzie That's three power cuts in three days. We can't go on having power cuts one after another like this.

Ted Lizzie. Wave.

She does so half-heartedly.

Ted Are you doing it?

Lizzie   Look Ted. Just start coming towards me and
            we'll meet in the middle.

They start crawling.

Lizzie   And don't forget you're looking for a candle!

Ted   Nothing yet. Hey, sis, does this not remind
            you of when we were small?

Lizzie   I walked from an early age Ted. Mother always
            said I started early.

Ted   That's not what I meant. I was thinking about
            me creeping up on you.

Lizzie   *(Does she remember?)* Yes.

Ted   I used to tell you that the Bogey Man was
            coming to get you... With his dark brown hair,
            rough beard and smell of stale cigarettes...

*TED finds the candle, pockets it and keeps crawling,
searching.*

Ted   I'd always manage to make you jump

wouldn't I?

Lizzie   Yes.

He's almost reached her, unnoticed by LIZZIE.

Ted   I'd always manage to make my little sister go three feet in the air...

He pounces.

Ted   BOO!

Lizzie   Ahh! Ted, for goodness sake!

Ted   *(Helpless with laughter)* Oh, oh... I could see you all the time! Your f-f-ace... Oh Lizzie!

Lizzie   This is no time for tricks. Where can that dratted candle be? You're sure... you're absolutely sure you dropped it?

He places it in her hand.

Ted   Found it two minutes ago.

Lizzie Thank goodness. I was beginning to wonder.

Finds a box of matches and fumbles to find one.
Strikes one and lights the candle.

Beat - They enjoy the flame.

Lizzie New candle too. That was worth all that
crawling about.

Ted No sign of anything stirring outside.

Lizzie Too early I suppose.

Ted Better go back to bed, I reckon. Safer there.

Lizzie Safer?

Ted Away from things that go bump in the night.

Lizzie Oh Ted. Well I'll stay down here. You go. It's
fine.

Ted You must be cold. Here.

Hands her his dressing gown. LIZZIE considers then
accepts and sits.

Lizzie   Thanks, Ted. No chance the heating's working I suppose?

Ted   None I'm afraid.

Lizzie   Just my rotten luck.

Ted   It's not just you.

Lizzie   Who else?

Ted   I lost the candle, didn't I? That's rotten luck.

Lizzie   *(A smile)* You always were the messy one. Clumsy.

Ted   Now wait a minute!

Lizzie   Father used to…

Ted   I lead an ordered life.

Lizzie   If you're ordered that makes me the world's most tidy person.

Ted   Now that's absolutely not true!

Lizzie   And you never tell the tiniest porky pies?

Ted   Me? Never! Straight as an arrow me. A lifetime as a teacher shows you that. Honesty is

something that you earn and that no matter
what the circumstances you always give.

Lizzie   So you never lied to a boy then?

Ted   Not once.

Lizzie   Even when they had no aptitude whatsoever
for academia but you just wanted them to
feel good.

Ted   That's encouragement. Totally different.

Lizzie   It's still an untruth.

Beat.

Lizzie   Oh for goodness sake!

Ted   It'll be back. It always comes back.

Lizzie   We need power.

Ted   What about...? Oh. I'm sorry Lizzie. If I hadn't
moved in maybe you'd have gone somewhere
smaller. A little bungalow or something instead
of us two rattling around here.

Lizzie   No Ted! This is my home. It may be coming
apart at the seams but it's where I lived with
Alan for almost thirty years. We bought it
with our life savings and he never stopped

loving this house until the day he died. When I leave this place it'll be... Well, a long time yet. *(Of candle)* Doesn't it warm your cockles?

Ted   It doesn't give out much heat.

Lizzie But it makes things seem better somehow. Perhaps that's just talking. A candle's so cosy, so romantic I suppose.

Ted   There were no more in the box.

Lizzie No more candles? See that just proves it, over the last few months with so many power cuts we've been careless. Used up our stock too quickly.

Ted   We'll have to be damned careful with this one.

Lizzie Yes, it's too treacherous to go outside. The path as it is, all crumbled after the storms. I tried last week but it was no good, no good at all.

Ted   Any requests before – ?

LIZZIE hasn't. TED blows out the flame.

Lizzie   I've a good mind to ring someone. But I've no idea who to call – and I doubt we could afford them anyway.

Ted   It has to be back on soon. What about a fire?

Lizzie   Yes, but what would we light it with?

Ted   *(Beat)* What about the turbine?!

Lizzie   Oh not this again. I've told you before it's a total disaster. The north wind could blow as hard as it liked and that thing would just stay still. It sways more from the bottom than the top.

Ted   I know that I could get it going again.

Lizzie   Ted. Honestly. It's never worked, not from the moment Alan constructed it. Lucky we never had to rely on it when he was alive. The electricity was fine then. I can't understand what's going on.

Ted   Well, that's why I've had a little idea –

Lizzie   And electricians are so expensive these days.

Ted   I couldn't find any manuals or instructions.

Lizzie   Ted! This is Alan we're talking about.

My husband may have been many things...
The kindest man on God's earth but he had
new fads like you drink cups of tea. And he
never read an instruction manual in his life,
let alone kept one.

Ted   But Alan said wind energy was going to
change everything. He was always banging
on about it. So...

Lizzie   Alan always thought everything was going to
change everything. And yes, it might if you've
got the right equipment. That thing's had it. It
was old before its time. Alan erected it the
month before he – *(It catches her.)*

Ted   Oh.

Lizzie   Rusty parts. Battered by the wind and rain.
Now it's stopped going round altogether. Bit
like us, eh?

Ted   Yes. But I was thinking, well, it would get us
out of a fix though, wouldn't it?

Lizzie   That's the trouble when you're an early
adopter. You're first off the starting blocks but
by the time the rest of the world catches up
you're puffed out. I'm telling you it's neither
use nor ornament.

Ted   I think that turbine could save us. Wouldn't Alan be proud?

Lizzie   You're welcome to try, Ted.

Ted   Well I think our problems are at an end, Lizzie.

TED goes.

Lizzie   That was Alan all over. Wonderful at starting something, not so good at the end.

She hides wiping away a tear and doesn't notice TED shuffle in with a length of old cooker hose which he connects (Heath Robinson-ish) to the exercise bike.

Ted   Ta-dah!

Lizzie   What's that Ted?

Ted   I said 'Ta-dah!'

Lizzie   What on earth do you mean?

Ted   I told you I've solved all of our problems Lizzie! Every single one.

Lizzie Have you even started on the boiler? You haven't, have you! You've been simply messing around with – with...
this nonsensical rubbish!

Ted Please. Lizzie. LISTEN!

Beat.

Ted I want to show you my invention. No. Don't say anything.

Lizzie What is it for heaven's sake?

He walks towards the exercise bike.

Ted Let me show you how it works first before you start making judgements.

Lizzie The turbine's not going round.

Ted That's because you're not pedalling on this.

Lizzie Pedalling... Me... On that thing? No.

Ted It'll warm you up.

Lizzie Sheer lunacy! I can't get on that thing. I'll break my neck! I'll –

Ted   Oh where's your spirit of adventure?

LIZZIE rather cautiously approaches the bike.

Lizzie   And this will solve our problems?

Ted   I promise.

LIZZIE takes several attempts to get onto the bike.
Eventually TED gives her a leg up. Finally she's on,
gripping the bike for dear life.

Ted   Now come on Lizzie start pedalling.

She does – slowly at first.

Lizzie   Nothing's happening... Is it... working?

Ted   You'll have to go faster than that.

LIZZIE responds with a quicker pace. As she pedals
the lights flash on and off.

Ted It's working! See that Lizzie, it's actually working!

TED walks towards the window and stares out. Smiling. LIZZIE's puffing and panting, trying to remove layers of clothing at the same time.

Ted Don't slow down! Keep those legs moving! Think of all that energy we're generating!

More clothes are coming off.

Ted What you need is a song! A good song for cycling! I know. How about 'It's A Long Way To Tipperary'?

Lizzie *(sings)*
Dai-sy! Dai-sy! Give me your answer do…

LIZZIE continues to sing over TED's speech.

Ted Yes that's it! Don't slow down. Keep those legs moving! It's like one of those wind-up radios. You need at least three hours of rotation to get five minutes of electricity.

It's totally fool proof!

LIZZIE is out of breath, exhausted.
She stops pedalling.

Ted   Lizzie!

She indicates that she can do no more and it is more
than TED's life is worth to ask her.

Ted   It's so easy and straightforward. I don't know
why I didn't think of it before!

LIZZIE's trying to get off but can't.

Ted   So what do you think? I think we could work
out a sort of rota system... You do mornings
say six 'til eleven.

She still can't dismount.

Lizzie   Would you give me a hand here? I'm a little
stuck.

Ted   Me afternoons say two 'til four and then take pot luck in the evening.

Lizzie Ted?

Ted   What do you say?

Lizzie Ted?

Ted   I think that's workable.

Lizzie TED! Will you please give me a hand!

Ted   Sorry sis.

He helps her off and she staggers to a chair. TED's rubbing his hands together.

Ted   See, I told you that you had no reason to worry. All our problems are at an end. It may have taken a while but finally –

Lizzie It will never work. We could never generate enough to keep us going.

Ted   Of course it will. It just did.

Lizzie Yes, with me puffing my lungs out. And we're still in the dark. Like asthmatic bats. We can't do that night and day Ted.

It's totally impractical.

Ted   At least it kept you warm. I'm freezing.

Lizzie   Well you've still done nothing whatsoever
with the boiler. I asked you over a week ago.

Ted   You're just down because the power's off. It's
bound to depress you.

Lizzie   I'd be better off with Alan.

Ted   You don't mean that.

She nods weakly.

Ted   A nice cup of something's what you need old
thing. Remember when we were small and
Mother used to give us boiled sweets. I'd do
anything for one of those at this moment. You
never finished yours.

Lizzie   I did. You were the one who always stopped
sucking halfway through. You got bored.

Ted   We had to hide them from Father.

Lizzie   Yes. So I'd end up popping it in my mouth,
just to avoid him getting angry and making

everything worse. Again.

Ted   You've always been there for me. Lizzie, I
          don't think I've ever really told you how
          much –

Lizzie I want no more excuses from you Ted.
          Tomorrow that boiler is paramount. I'll be
          checking your work.

Ted   My top priority Lizzie.

Lizzie You seem to think this is all a great game. See
          those curtains? I made those out of a summer
          dress. When I think of when I was a little girl.
          Mother and Father always seemed to have
          money to spare didn't they?

Ted   Yes. I suppose we were lucky. In some ways.

Lizzie I won't wear anything nice ever again I dare
          say. Needs must I'm afraid. If I could afford a
          man to come out and fix the boiler, I would.

Ted   I wanted to do something right. Something
          good.

Lizzie The best thing you can do with that
          contraption is pull it down. I've told you
          before it's useless. I told Alan that when he
          was constructing the thing. Dream on, I said.

Fine, have thirty of the things in the middle of
the sea but here? What we need is something
practical. Enough talking. Action this day!

Beat.

Ted   I might head up to Bedfordshire. It'll be
warmer there.

Beat.

Lizzie   It was me who told you about the Bogey
Man, you know. You got that wrong earlier.

Ted   No it wasn't. I told you. I'm the eldest. I
invented him. /

Lizzie   Oh no you did not!

Ted   The man who snatches little girls in the
middle of the night when they haven't been
kind to their big brother.

Lizzie   That's rubbish Ted and you know it.

Ted   Of course it's rubbish. I made him up.

Lizzie   For the last time, you did not.

Ted   Why do you care so much? It's just a silly
story.

Lizzie I believed it. I believed every word my big brother said in those days.

Ted Of course you did. Well just forget it now, will you? Those sort of things are best left well alone.

Lizzie It's going to snow. I can feel it.

Ted That's all we need. All the more reason to get that turbine going.

Lizzie Well just be careful out there. I saw what it was like.

Ted It can't be that bad surely!

Lizzie I would hate anything to happen to you.

Ted It's fine.

Lizzie When I did venture out... it wasn't the landscape I remembered somehow. In my mind's eye I saw green, lush grass but it was brown. All sludgy brown.

Ted You're being silly.

Lizzie You didn't see it.

Ted Lizzie, I promise. That turbine is going to solve all our problems.

Lizzie   Just take care that's all. You promise?

He fumbles for her hand in the darkness. Holds it for a while as they stare into the blackness. Then TED finds new energy.

Ted   Fancy a dance?

Lizzie   A dance?!

Ted   Yes.

Lizzie   A dance?!

Ted   That's what I said.

Lizzie   You must be running a temperature.

Ted   It would be fun. It would keep us warm. What do you say to a saucy rumba?

Lizzie   It's utter lunacy. Even if we did manage to shuffle our way round, how would we see?

Ted   You can dance in the dark. Who needs to see? We'll feel our way round the room. We'll use each other for support.

Lizzie   No.

Ted Oh go on little sis. It'll be fun. I promise. Just a little... Look we can do it right here... Now... What earthly reason why not?

LIZZIE relents – stands up.

Lizzie So?

Ted Your hands. Where are they?

LIZZIE finds his hands and TED puts her into hold. They're ready...

Lizzie Music. Surely we need something to dance to!

Ted Yes. Where's the candle?

Lizzie Why?

Ted *(Absently)* That old gramophone's a wind-up isn't it? Alan's records... There's bound to be something.

LIZZIE snaps out of hold.

Lizzie   No.

Ted   But Lizzie... I – /

Lizzie   I said no. I meant no.

Ted   But honestly, they'd be properly...

Lizzie   You're not to touch Alan's record collection.
As long as you're in this house.

Ted   Truly I promise.

Lizzie   No! I told you that when you came to live
here, Ted. I said, Alan's collection is out of
bounds. My final word, Ted.

Silence.

*TED stares into space, visibly smarting. LIZZIE pulls
the dressing gown round her tightly. She breathes it in,
and cries softly. TED puts his hand out for hers and
she finds it.*

Lizzie   Don't.

Ted   I'm sorry. Really.

Lizzie   I shouldn't have lost my temper. It's just...

Everything's bubbling just below the surface. And most days I manage to keep it simmering and some days I boil over. And when I hear music... It's as though someone is plucking at my heart but not gently. They're beating it to a pulp.

Ted   Let's forget it shall we?

Lizzie   It's no excuse. I should never have snapped. It was unforgivable.

Ted   Ha! That's nothing. I've seen you really go for the jugular.

Lizzie   Don't joke Ted please.

Ted   I wasn't.

Lizzie   When Alan died I thought if I kept the records just as they were then I'd never have to deal with it. A refuge if you like.

Ted   Please. Lizzie.

Lizzie   I want to talk about it. He was so protective of them. And there were times... Cataloguing and re-cataloguing... I could have put each one over my knee and smashed them one after another.

Ted   But you didn't. (*Beat*) I can't feel my toes and the end of my nose is but a distant memory. I've had enough. I'm going to... to... I'm going to walk up and down.

Lizzie   You'll bump into things.

Ted   Well then I'll jog on the spot.

Lizzie   You'll get out of breath.

Ted   Alright then I'll –

LIZZIE's found the candle and the matches. She lights it, carefully.

Ted   But the candle...

She goes to the shelves of records and pulls one out.

Lizzie   Just this once.

She dusts off the player and puts the record on and winds it up. An old classic (perhaps 'Let's Face The Music and Dance?') fills the air.

Lizzie Would you care to dance, Mr Stevens?

Ted I'm meant to say that. I'd be delighted Mrs
Kirkpatrick...

*LIZZIE realises the candle's a hindrance and blows it
out. In the darkness they slip easily into hold. They
dance tentatively, without much grace at first but then
slowly they get into their stride.*

Ted You know for a mere shuffler you're not bad.

Lizzie Thank you. Perhaps it's because you can't see
me that it helps.

Ted Maybe that's it!

The lights snap on. The power is back.
*The ridiculousness of the situation is immediately
apparent to LIZZIE and TED.*
The music continues as before.

Lizzie Oh.

Ted Look at us. Silly old things!

Lizzie   Yes.

Ted   *(Stopping dancing.)* Yes.

Lizzie   *(Wanting to keep going)* Thank goodness.

Ted   Bed then.

Lizzie   Yes, although we could... Just a little longer.

She tries to dance again but TED is rigid.

Lizzie   Oh come on Ted. You said this would be fun
and it is.

Ted   *(Heading off)* Tea then first I think!

Lizzie   Ted. Please don't go yet. The song's not even
over. Please.

He turns to her.

Lizzie   One last waltz?

*He smiles. Goes to her. They are in hold again.
They begin a more confident dance. Then the music*

dies on the gramophone as it runs out of steam.

The lights fade.

The turbine clatters its way round to 'half past'...

TWO

Winter. Christmas Day. Morning.

There is a thin layer of snow on the ground but it is light despite a cold sky and ominous black clouds. There is light from a single bulb but it is still a stark contrast from the previous scene. The living room now looks as though LIZZIE and TED are using very little of the rest of the house. The room is dotted with buckets and boxes. Both are in sleeping bags and are fully clothed with bobble hats. In the corner of the room a single spindly branch has been strewn with homemade decorations. TED is awake but LIZZIE looks fast asleep. He creeps round, looking for something. He takes a peep through the curtains.

Lizzie   *(In her sleep)* Mmm...

TED jumps. Stands still. Then continues searching.

Lizzie   I hope you're not doing what I think you are.

Ted   Course not.

Lizzie   Because you won't find them you know.

Ted   I wouldn't dare.

Lizzie   'Course you wouldn't.

Ted   Happy Christmas!

He kisses her.

Lizzie   *(Kisses him back)* Happy Birthday!

Ted   Thanks. Another year and all that.

Lizzie   I was always so jealous of you when we were small.

Ted   Why for heaven's sake?

Lizzie   Double the celebration. Who wouldn't be green?

Ted   Mother and Father tried to make it special for both of us every year. And it's not all it's cracked up to be either. If I'm honest it was I who was really jealous of you.

Lizzie   I don't remember.

Ted   Yes you do. You used to play on it for months on end that you had your own special day. A birthday all to yourself and I had to share

mine with everyone – and Jesus! See. So
there's really nothing to be jealous of then.

LIZZIE gets up.

Lizzie Do you want them then? I'm going to empty
the bucket first. The roof's leaking so much.

Ted Oh.

*She goes. TED continues his frantic search. LIZZIE's
soon back with an empty bucket.*

Lizzie Now please don't get too excited...
It's nothing earth shattering... things being...
as they are.

*She starts pulling records enthusiastically (but respect-
fully) out of shelves searching for something behind.*

Lizzie I think I have really cracked the hiding place
this year!

TED's watching her. His look screams 'no!'

Lizzie   Even I was pleased. I thought 'he'll never dare to look here!'

Ted   Oh goodness!

Lizzie   You can of course hide things too well.

Ted   Lizzie! I've just noticed. It's amazing! The electricity. Have you noticed the power is on?

LIZZIE stops. The presents are forgotten.

Lizzie   My God. Ted! My God! Yes!

They cling to each other.

Lizzie   I feel like... I don't know! Well waking up with actual light. I don't know... I feel like... what should we do first Ted?

TED's eyeing the shelves.

Lizzie Ted?

Ted Well whatever it is we'd better be quick.

Lizzie *(Paralysed)* Yes. I know, I know... I can't think what to do first! Is that funny? Oh this will be the best Christmas ever!

Ted *(Trying to get rid of her)* And it's white.

Lizzie A white Christmas!

Ted Well a little. It's certainly not deep and crisp and even but it'll still be very beautiful. Why don't you go out and look at it?

Lizzie Out there – me? I'm not going out there! I'll be dead in seconds. No Ted!

Ted There's always the window.

Lizzie Don't touch those curtains. We'll lose the little heat we have.

Ted *(Desperate)* What about a birthday breakfast for your brother?

Lizzie What about it?

Ted Using the *electric* cooker!

Lizzie I'll go and see what there is.

TED watches her go and then frantically starts searching the shelves. Eventually, he finds a wad of letters – where can he hide them? LIZZIE enters unseen, carrying a Fray Bentos Pie.

Lizzie Last one. Birthday breakfast or Christmas dinner?

Ted Ah.

Lizzie Those aren't my parcels. Mine are in newspaper. I used old sheets and old string too. I hope you managed to recycle something. I shan't mind at all. In fact I'd be pleased. Who's been writing to you?

Ted No-one.

Lizzie Well those must be from someone. What are they then? A secret?

Ted Yes! No. Just circulars. I was just about to throw them out.

Lizzie I'll do it.

Ted No! Don't do that. Sit down. It's Christmas. I'll –

Lizzie Honestly. I may as well bin them as I'm

heading to the kitchen.

Ted These should go straight outside. Don't want them getting mixed up with any birthday or Christmas cards.

Lizzie Not that I've seen a single one. You're being very protective.

Ted They're private. Anyway, I haven't had my presents yet!

Lizzie No-one would ever believe that you were the eldest.

Ted Meaning?

Lizzie You can sometimes behave just like a spoilt child!

Ted Well, I'm very sorry.

Lizzie No, no. It's your birthday.

Ted You're right. Let's be grown up.

Lizzie First time for everything.

LIZZIE snatches the letters.

Ted   Lizzie!

LIZZIE stares. TED can't look at her.

Lizzie *(Quiet. Barely controlled)* What are these?
            They're addressed to me. What are they? *(She
            tears one open.)* From the electricity board?
            This one's from months ago. I don't
            understand. We can't owe... not all this? It's
            too much. I just thought we'd been paying. I
            thought there was enough money in the
            account. I am such a bloody fool! No wonder
            the postman never came...
            Except he did, didn't he? Now I know why
            you were so desperate to get that turbine
            going.

Beat.

            I wanted this to be such a nice day. Different
            to the other days. Why have you done this?
            You coward... you're selfish, heartless!
            (Tearing open envelopes.) Red, red, red, red,
            red! Are there more?

TED shakes his head.

All I thought of was you. And what did you
think of? You. Thousands! Here we are day
after day tearing off tiny bits of paper for the
loo. When we can't afford food, heating,
lighting!

Ted   Let me speak! Please.

Suddenly LIZZIE runs to the light switch.

Lizzie   All expense!

*LIZZIE touches the switch and gets a massive electric
shock, with a flash and bang.*

She cries out. The lights go out.

Ted   Lizzie! Lizzie! Oh God!

Lizzie   Water! Help me.

Ted   The pipes are frozen.

Lizzie   Kettle!

TED fumbles for the kettle. LIZZIE manages to find a

package, rips it open with one hand. Ted's birthday present – the one she was making. LIZZIE puts water on the jumper and wraps it round her hand. LIZZIE breathes.

Lizzie   *(Indicating jumper)* You won't be needing this.

Ted   Are you alright?

Lizzie   *(Deflated)* How can one feel so good one moment and the next...?

Ted   It was one letter at first. It was addressed to you. I couldn't believe how much it was for. And I didn't know what to do. You were so sad. Grieving. It was just the wrong time to bring up a stupid bill. And then another came. And a reminder for the first one. And then another. All this money. And I just didn't know how to tell you. What you owed. I tried to help. But I didn't have enough. And then all the rain. The roof leaking. Then the boiler. Another reminder. I just. Couldn't cope. Just. Embarrassed and. I didn't know what to do. I just thought you didn't need to worry about that. After Alan –

Lizzie   Don't mention his name. He was too good for

you.

Ted   You must understand. Seeing you like that –

Lizzie   I'll tell you why I've been unhappy, shall I? Because for the last year I've been on my hands and knees, crawling from day to day. I asked you here because I thought you felt the same. I thought you'd know that feeling because of Carl. At least because of him.

Deadly silence.

Lizzie   When you've lost someone, the thing you need most is your family. And trust, always trust. Isn't that right Ted?

Ted   Carl has nothing to do with this. He's not relevant.

Lizzie   Your son is as relevant on this day as he was ten years ago.

Ted   No.

Lizzie   It's Christmas Ted, and whether you like it or not he runs through everything you do. He's the blood in your veins but you won't talk about him. Won't have his picture up.

Ted   This is about you and me.

Lizzie   This is about Carl too. You hide him away
inside you just as you did with those letters
because you're unable to face the real world.
Or the truth, Ted.

Ted   No.

Lizzie   The truth is that he's dead. We both know that.

Ted   I have never denied my son. That's the truth,
Lizzie. As God is my witness that is the truth.

Lizzie   All your life you've been running away,
putting on fronts. All the time trying to be
what Father wanted you to be but never were.
What happened to the little boy who wanted
to climb mountains and see far-off places?

Ted   I've always been me.

Lizzie   No Ted, you've always been what you thought
you should be. The great teacher and now my
protector. You thought you should hide the
truth in case it was too great. I'm beginning to
wonder if you're even capable of telling the
truth.

Ted   I did it for you, how many times? I couldn't
tell you. I. Didn't want to tell you.

Lizzie   You're more like Father than you think.

Ted   I'm nothing like him.

Lizzie   That's why I loved Alan – he was the pure antithesis of Father.

Ted   And of course he always told the truth.

Lizzie   What about that day ten years ago Ted? When I had to tell you about Carl.

Ted   Please.

Lizzie   Do you think I wanted to knock on your door and tell a man whose wife had just left him that his son...

Ted   Lizzie.

Lizzie   … was dead. And I could have lied. I could have said they'd found him in hospital, rather than on some street corner, living hand to mouth from a cardboard box.

Ted   He chose to run away.

Lizzie   I could have told a little white lie to make it easier but I knew that I would hurt you more if one day you found out the truth. Ted I would never have been able to look my brother in the face again so I did the hardest thing imaginable.

Pause as TED cries softly into his hands. LIZZIE moves to the window.
She stares.

Lizzie What might it be like to lose yourself in snow? To simply open the door one morning, put on your coat and your hat and walk... Just slowly. Walk into the snow as the flakes fall. Then when you've gone as far as you can you just stand, perfectly still, and stare out into the distance... When you've stood there for a long time and the snow has piled itself up, risen well above your waist, the weight of it forces you forwards. You find yourself lying face down. Your pink, tired face against the startling white of the snow. You imagine that you'd fight it. Try to get up.

Ted Lizzie?

Lizzie But of course you don't. You just lie there in the cold. Surrendered. Until you begin to feel quite warm. And the flakes keep falling and falling. And you don't notice because you're gone completely and when they find you it's all too late. That would be a way to go.

She moves off towards the door. Puts on her coat and hat and goes. Ted sits, defeated.

After some moments she comes back.

Lizzie   *(Anguished)* It wasn't deep enough.

LIZZIE is broken. She sits. TED goes to speak. He can't. Finally TED gets up, finds the present.

Ted   *(Holding out the parcel)* This is from me.

She won't take it.

Ted   It's not much but it's Christmas.

She still won't take it or acknowledge him. He unwraps the present. It is a miner's lamp. TED turns it on.

Blackout.

The turbine inches round to 'quarter to', grinding and clanking as it does so...

THREE

Spring. The snow is thicker. The house is darker than ever and a low wind is whistling.

The room is much the same but all of the records have been shelved again and there are piles of books all over the place with titles like 'Renewables and How They Work' etc. LIZZIE and TED now only have the miner's lamp – meaning that they must stay as close as they can within its beam or be left in darkness.

There is a noticeable change in TED and LIZZIE's physical appearance. TED has started using a stick and LIZZIE is stooping more but is keeping up appearances for TED's sake. However, there is a definite sense of decline during this scene – every movement is an effort for LIZZIE and TED; they should get closer and closer to the ground. There is a feral quality to them.

TED is under a blanket sitting on his sleeping bag. He finds a tin of rice pudding and a spoon with obvious delight. Begins to open it.

Lizzie   *(Off. Lots of effort)* Ted! Ted! Come and give me a hand will you?

Ted   I'm busy.

Lizzie *(Off)* Ted!

Ted Lizzie. I said I'm busy.

Lizzie *(Off)* Please Ted. I need you.

Ted Alright. I'm coming, I'm coming!

He hides the tin and goes to help her.

Ted What is it?

Lizzie *(Off. Straining)* You take that end.

Ted *(Off. Even more effort)* Of that thing! I thought you'd given up on it.

Lizzie *(Off)* It's the only way.

Ted *(Off)* If I couldn't get it to work...

Lizzie *(Off)* We'll never know if we don't try will we? One – two – three.

Ted *(Off)* They have cranes to do this you know.

Lizzie *(Off)* Just lift it.

They half lift, half drag one of the blades from the turbine. It is excruciating to watch as both struggle but

*they are determined. They manage to get the tip
sticking into the room. LIZZIE looks exhausted and is
wearing the miner's lamp.*

Lizzie   More! It needs to come through more.

Ted   Sorry...! No can do.

Lizzie   But Ted.

Ted   I'm all in. How the hell...? I need to sit down.
How the hell did you get it down?

Lizzie   A system of ropes and pulleys.

Ted   Good grief.

He sits down.

Lizzie   But it'll have to come further into the house if
I'm to work on it properly.

Ted   Can't be done.

Lizzie   No?

Ted   Just work on it there.

Lizzie   *(Giving in)* Fine.

Ted   I don't know what you think you're doing. Over a month of being outside in all hours, banging about.

Lizzie   This has to work Ted. It has to. Before this place collapses around us. How else are we going to survive?

Ted   I know but can't you just stop for a moment?

Lizzie   No this has to be back on the turbine before tonight.

She begins to work on the turbine blade, kneeling. He's eating, unseen by LIZZIE.

Ted   How long are we expected to cope, left to live like this! It's the limit, it really is. I can't take much more.

Lizzie   It's my stomach if I'm honest that I'm most aware of. Trying to eke our food out. Making sure that both of us are fed, that we don't starve. And we're down to the last few tins.

He's just dipping his spoon when she catches him.

Lizzie   Ted?

Ted   Yes.

Lizzie   Where did you get that?

Ted   Found it.

Lizzie   Where did you find it?

Ted   Nowhere.

Lizzie   Ted. Please. Can I have some?

Ted   It's mine.

Lizzie   Ted please. I need it. I'm starving.

Ted   Well I'm not giving you any.

He starts shoving it quickly into his mouth.

Lizzie   Give it to me.

Ted   *(Eating more)* Sorry.

Lizzie   Ted. I didn't eat anything at all yesterday.

She tries to grab it – desperately – but he's too quick for her. He stops.

Lizzie   Is there more? Where have you been hiding them? Show me.

Ted   No.

LIZZIE lunges for the tin and they scrap over it intensely like children – desperate for it. In the end LIZZIE manages to get the spoon only.

Lizzie   You...!

Beat.

Ted   Do you think anyone will ever find us, Lizzie? The authorities. Social services.

Lizzie   I hope not. They can't. If anyone does, you will say we're fine won't you Ted? That we can manage?

Ted   But surely it would be nice to see someone once in a while. Just for a bit. Sometimes I wake up at night in a cold sweat.

Lizzie   But what if that person knows how much we owe. We can never pay it back, ever. We'd have to live for another hundred years! I live in fear that one day soon someone important will come knocking on that door. It could happen any day and / then

Ted   Then we might be separated.

Lizzie   No Ted! *(Going back to the blade)* Give me a
hand with this will you?

Ted   Sorry Lizzie. I don't think I can. Please stop
for a moment.

Lizzie   No time.

Ted   Please.

Lizzie   I said no time Ted.

Ted   Lizzie –

Lizzie   I'm not giving up. Father always said I would
never be anyone. Well –

Ted   Oh. Dear Lizzie, it doesn't matter now.

Lizzie   No. Not now. But it did when we were small
and he made us stand to attention.
And I shook. Then it mattered.

Ted   He did love you.

Lizzie   You can't buy love though, can you?

Ted   And God knows he tried.

Lizzie   Pocket money after he'd shouted. To make
things better... Now are you going to help or
aren't you?

Beat.

Lizzie   Right then, brother. I shall move it on my
own. One... two... three!

She lifts. It moves and hits her leg.

Lizzie   Ow! Ow!

Ted   Lizzie! Oh dear, oh dear!

Lizzie   Ow! Why do these things keep happening to
me?

Ted   Just sit there and rest for a moment. And if I
see you moving, there'll be hell to pay.

*LIZZIE gives in. She sits. LIZZIE is quiet. She closes her
eyes, and nods off a little.*

The wind slowly builds.

LIZZIE wakes with a start from her sleep, scared.

Lizzie Ted!

Ted What is it?

Lizzie I thought I saw... I'm cold.

Ted Are you alright? Is it your shin?

Lizzie Cold.

He gives her a blanket. She dozes off again until...

Lizzie Ted?

Ted Yes? What is it?

Lizzie Mouth's dry.

Ted Yes. Can you wait?

Lizzie Mouth Ted.

*He fills up a glass with rainwater from the bucket –
what harm can it do? Gives it to her. Sits.*

Lizzie Ted?

Ted What?

Lizzie   Thank you.

Ted   You're welcome. Now you get some rest. *(Yawns.)*

Lizzie   You need some rest too.

Ted   I'm fine. Fit as an ox me.

Lizzie   Ted?

Ted   Mmm?

Lizzie   There's icicles on the end of your nose.

Ted   Really? *(Pretending)* Oh yes. Look at that! Eugh, a big one!

Lizzie   Ted, that's not an icicle!

They laugh. TED shivers. Moments pass.

The wind whistles.

LIZZIE drifts off then wakes with a start.

Lizzie   Ted! It's happening again!

Ted   What's happening?

Lizzie   The tree.

Ted   What tree, Lizzie?

Lizzie   The oak tree. It's going to fall.

Ted   That'll never fall.

Lizzie   I saw it move. It's going to fall.

Ted   It won't. I promise. I've never seen a more
              sturdy-looking tree.

Lizzie   It'll crash down – onto us.

Ted   Nothing bad is going to happen.

Lizzie   You can't be sure.

Ted   I'm your brother. Trust me.

Lizzie   I did.

Ted   You have always had an overactive
              imagination. Ever since we were little. Like
              the blessed Bogey Man.

Lizzie   *(Too tired)* You told me about the Bogey Man.

Ted   Yes.

Lizzie   He wasn't a story. He was real.

Ted   Don't be silly!

Lizzie   The beard. The funny clothes, the smell. The way he took children in the night. Us. Lifted them up into his arms and... put them back into bed again.

Ted   I don't understand.

Lizzie   I saw him too. As clearly as I see you now. Did you never wonder why he never did us any real harm? Why he came in sometimes at night when he wasn't posted away?

Ted   Father?

Lizzie   I hated him, you know.

There's a loud crash (a tile falls from the roof.)
They both jump.

Lizzie   It's happened! I knew it would. I told you!

Ted   *(Rushing to the window.)* It's not the tree. It looks like another roof tile's blown off. Oh no.

Beat.

Lizzie   At least you had Carl. You miss him don't you?

Ted   Yes.

Lizzie   What else is there to do when you're stuck at
             our age but think about the past? About the
             people who are lost.

Ted   I haven't. Not until the last few months. Since
             I found the albums of him as a little boy.

Lizzie   Have them out.

Ted   No point. He's gone.

Lizzie   Even more reason.

Ted   Perhaps.

Lizzie   What about me? You had a son. You should
             be so proud.

Ted   Oh.

Lizzie   Alan was many things. Endless wonderful
             things but not that. He couldn't do that. You
             must have Carl's photographs on display.
             However things were at the end he's still
             worth remembering.

Ted   You won't mind?

Lizzie   He's my nephew! I'd love it.

Ted   Thanks.

Lizzie   Go on then. The album!

TED goes to fetch it.

Lizzie   You're shivering.

Ted   Well it has got colder.

Lizzie   *(Of album)* Let's see then!

Ted   Right well... Oh look his first day at school.

Lizzie   He does look so smart in that uniform.

Ted   And look here... That train set. Gosh that takes me back.

Lizzie   Oh look. That's you!

Ted   It's us.

Lizzie   Don't look very happy do we? Fishing trip. Never my favourite.

Ted   Like everything, rather a boot camp with Father.

Lizzie   Did you enjoy those trips Ted?

Ted   No. Days of enforced fun are never a good idea.

He starts looking at more photographs.

Lizzie   *(Sings)*

You shall have a fishy on a little dishy
You shall have a fishy when the boat comes in
You shall have a herring on a little dishy
You shall have a herring when the boat comes in.

Dance to your Daddy my little laddie...
(Sotto) Dance to your Daddy my little man.
Dance to your... daddy...

Ted   What was that?

Lizzie   I don't know. It just came back to me. How come I can remember that but I never seem to know what day it is.

She shakes her head a little.

Ted   *(Of brazier)* I could light the fire. Save the candle.

Lizzie   What with? There's no wood.

Ted   There's a little wood from Christmas.

Lizzie   That twig? *(Wry)* We'll have to be careful it doesn't take our eyebrows off.

TED looks at the photographs. Starts removing photos from album. He scrunches one up. Repeats. Places them in the brazier. Starts hunting round for matches. LIZZIE sees as he brings them back to the brazier. Takes out more photos.

Lizzie   Ted?

Ted   Why not, eh Lizzie? Why not?

Lizzie   Ted. You can't. Carl –

Ted   Carl isn't in here. He's in here – in my heart.

Lizzie   But you can't. Please don't!

Ted   I won't forget him.

Lizzie   It's wrong Ted.

Ted   You and me we're here now and if I have to spend one more sodding day with every part of my body cold, straining to see even the tiniest crack of light, then I might just go mad.

TED is tearing the photos. They're both on their knees.

Lizzie Don't Ted, please!

Ted I'd eat them if I could. If it would stop my stomach from hurting so much.

Lizzie Just stop please!

Ted I'd rather break my heart than spend another hour like this.

Lizzie I'd rather turn myself in to Social Services!

Ted You know what will happen. Put into awful day centres and we'll never see each other again. I don't want to die alone.

Lizzie No!

Ted Is that what you want?

Lizzie Of course not but –

Ted I don't want to freeze to death either.

TED strikes a match.

Ted   *(Burns himself)* Ow!

Lizzie   Ted!

Ted   Let me do it my way.

LIZZIE knocks the matches from his hand. He rushes after them.

Trips. Falls. Lands with a heavy thud. The wind is a cacophony now surrounding them.

Lizzie   Ted? Ted?

She crawls towards him. Cries.

Are you alright? Oh God. Oh please God, make him be alright. Ted. Speak to me!

Blackout.

The turbine clatters round to the hour as bright sunshine appears...

FOUR

Summer.

Evening, dusk. There are new bulbs in the lamps. Everything now seems too bright. The room looks a little more organised and there are photos of Carl mixed in with Alan's. TED and LIZZIE are sat in their chairs squinting against the light. LIZZIE's wrapped up and TED has an arm in plaster. Both are wearing clean clothes.

Ted What's the time?

Lizzie About half past.

Ted Oh God.

Lizzie We could try hiding.

Ted It's no good. I tried that the other day.
She found me immediately, thought I was playing some sort of game. The dreaded Mrs 'Mop-It-Up'.

Lizzie There are worse than her.

Ted Are you sure?

Lizzie No.

Ted Exactly.

Lizzie   But it was one of Doctor's conditions.
A proper care package.

Ted   I know, I know. A trial period to see how we
adjust. I don't know what there is to adjust
to – it's our home after all.

Lizzie   Still it's better than nothing.

Ted   Suppose. Didn't like having to plead though.

Lizzie   But we won. That's all that matters. Though if
she starts having to take me to the toilet.

Ted   I'll shoot you first don't you worry.

Lizzie   Good. *(Wryly)* I'll see you up there.

Beat.

Lizzie   I can't believe that man got the turbine going.

Ted   Not sure I like the idea of selling our energy
back to the grid. Feels a bit dirty somehow.

Lizzie   You haven't forgotten how much we owe
have you? I still can't quite believe it's going
round. I keep looking up to check I'm not
dreaming. Alan would –
Sorry.

Ted   What is it?

Lizzie   I know that you don't like me talking about
him.

Ted   Oh Lizzie. You must talk about him.

Lizzie   Really?

Ted   You must gabble away as much as you want to.

Lizzie   *(Laughs)* I will. I promise. He'd have been so
proud. Finally one of his pet projects actually
making a difference. That's really something.
(Squinting against the light) Gosh this light's
bright.

Ted   Isn't it? I have to say I can't quite get used to it.

Lizzie   I know what you mean. Light whenever you
want it. Heating whenever you choose. It's not
natural.

Ted   It's no fun anymore.

Lizzie   Well...

Ted   Are you thinking what I'm thinking?

Lizzie   I think I might be, Ted Stevens. I might be.

TED eases himself out of his chair.

Ted   Ready?

Switches the light off with a satisfying click.

Ted   There.

Lizzie Oh now that's much better. *(Handing him a woolly hat.)* Here.

She puts one on herself.

Ted   Excellent. I'll get that fire going in a moment – with all that wood *she* found.

Lizzie At least that's one use then.

Ted   Yes. I turned the heating off earlier.

Lizzie Good. Awful waste of money. I can't stand it.

Ted   Oh.

Lizzie What?

Ted   Just one other thing.

Lizzie Careful.

Gets up on his chair and removes the bulb.

Ted   Hold me. Yes, yes.

Lizzie   Well done Ted.

The room returns to a semi-state of darkness.

Ted   *(Hiding it in his pocket) She*'ll never know.
Now, where's the candle?

LIZZIE reaches out for the – by now – stubby candle.

Lizzie   Here.

Ted   You'll have to light it.

LIZZIE does so.

Ted   So, old girl, fancy a dance?

Lizzie   Like I am?

Ted   No excuses this time.

Lizzie   Oh alright. I might manage a totter round.

Ted   I'm afraid you'll have to take charge of putting the record on.

Lizzie   If you give me a hand?

She goes to the record player, winds and places a record on, puts the needle down.

The same music plays as earlier. They get into position.

LIZZIE blows out the candle and they sway in time to the music.

As they dance the turbine silently does a full rotation.

Blackout.

END

BEHIND THE SCENES

An interview between
editor
Nadia Kingsley
and
playwright
Tom Wentworth

NK: *Windy Old Fossils… where did the idea come from?*

TW: I think I wanted to write about old people living in the countryside because it was a young writers' festival and I thought it would be good to have a play about the elderly in a festival I was sure would be full of young people's stories.

I don't know where the title came from. But once I had the title I thought 'I've got to come up with a play to go with it.'

Originally it was a four-actor comedy about a kidnap. Ted and Lizzie kidnap a neighbour and hold her to ransom so that her husband will get them on the mains electric. Something like that anyway.

NK: *Where did the idea of fuel shortages come from?*

TW: That's something I wanted to do. Had we been to that talk by then?

NK: *Oh – the marquee where we were asked to read, and the whole thing was raising money for their anti-wind turbines campaign?*

TW: I think something lodged there. It was a nice metaphor about both the elderly and fossil fuels – running out of energy, out of steam.

It was a composite of a lot of different things.

NK: *And rural living was because of Pentabus?*

TW: Yes, and everyone did write about rural living – but I think that's just because that is where we were all living, and where I had grown up…

NK: *You have always been good thinking about what a particular theatre company might need – I think this might have been the first time you did this?*

TW: Yes… and we weren't given any restriction. We were told 'just go off and write' and that's what came out.

NK: *Tell me about the different drafts you wrote.*

TW: I don't really remember the first four-actor draft. I guess it still exists somewhere. Everyone else had their notes on their first draft at the next Pentabus session, but I didn't – they ran out of time – so I had to go home without them. And the following week I was in London on another writers' development programme, so Simon Longman and I met up there.

Simon felt I should lose two characters and turn it into Ted and Lizzie's story, and I said "Great idea, but I only have two weeks to rewrite this completely before the rehearsals start."

But I went home and thought 'These are good notes'… they wanted me to develop Ted and Lizzie and concentrate more on fossil fuel: things that I had wanted to concentrate on but I hadn't really got to on that first draft – as you so often don't… but they had picked out *exactly* what I had wanted to say. So I couldn't ignore the notes. But at the same time I was terrified because of the time limitation. I really only had time for one shot at it, maybe two if I was really quick, so I turned it round really quickly. There can only have been one or two drafts of the new play…

NK: *Why did you feel, as a young man and an only child, that you could write about older siblings? Did you encounter any difficulties because of this and is there anything better in the play, do you think, because of your perspective?*

TW: Well, I didn't ever think I *couldn't* write about them.. they turned up like that.
And of course originally I wasn't writing about their story – I was writing about four people. By the time I got to Lizzie and Ted's own draft I was writing about them for a second time and I found they had fully formed.

NK: *I think it's amazing how you got the language so right.*

TW: Well, I had grandparents who I spent a lot of

time with.

NK: *Were they siblings?*

TW: No... so I guess I made that part up. But they did just come fully formed. And the other two characters in the first draft were quite cartoony – I think that's what Simon and Elizabeth picked up on.

That's what we do as writers isn't it? Imagine. And of course the actors were hugely helpful because they brought their own experiences, and questions.

NK: *So you rewrote in rehearsal?*

TW: I hardly rewrote because there wasn't much time. It sounds glib, I know, but it was all just there. Lizzie and Ted don't really share memories... We *think* they are remembering childhood memories but they aren't remembering the same things – and we all know what *that* is like in families.

Maybe that's it... I just wrote them as family rather than as siblings. And because they were older they had had whole lives separate from each other. There had been a child. Their concerns were about the young generation ie *my generation* – so I could write about that because I was living it. Lizzie and Ted are either talking about themselves or young people – and they are talking about the present time because they are still in crisis and still very present in their own lives.

Maybe being younger I bring a sense of hope about the older people, that wouldn't be there with an older playwright.

At the end of the play we know they carry on. I mean we know that they will die at some point of course… but not in the lifespan of the play.

NK: *Tell me about the young writers' group? What was the application process and how do you think the scheme helped you long term?*

TW: Well, the scheme helped me by putting a play on stage with actors, and giving us a deadline. And then I had a play as a calling-card-script and that got me an agent.

And a lot of industry people saw it who have given me wonderful opportunities.

Elizabeth had to decide which of the plays she was going to direct. I had been waiting and waiting to see who was going to direct *Windy Old Fossils* and then Elizabeth said 'I am going to direct it' – and I was so thrilled because I couldn't be there all the time but knew it would be in safe hands, and Simon was going to be there too, as dramaturg.

NK: *And the application process and the scheme?*

TW: I can't remember what the application process was like. The group met every three weeks for about nine months. We had masterclasses, and actors came in, then suddenly the festival was upon us.

NK: *And when you say actors came in – was that to read your plays?*

TW: I don't think we had started writing at that stage – so they were reading anything. Just to get the idea. All the other writers were very new.

NK: *And what kind of masterclasses were there?*

TW: We had a masterclass with the playwright Phil Porter. He was really good. And a masterclass with Francesca Millican-Slater; and then we had Simon and Elizabeth running the group – Simon was the Channel Four playwright-in-residence – they both took writers' workshops... all the things I had come to know from other groups. It was good fun. Oh, and we did audio plays that were set up like a map around Ludlow.

NK: *Tell me about the unseen characters …why is there Alan and why is there Carl? And why is there only a tiny mention of Ted's wife – who died?*

TW: Well, the wife thing is because it happened in the past. It happened and it's accepted. That's what goes on in a family, isn't it?... We know she is dead but we don't need to mention it all the time but we never forget it, in a family.

And then there's this son Carl. And there have obviously been issues there – leaving home, running away. It felt important that Ted had that *other* life that we knew about that came before this place and being elderly – and the same with Lizzie and Alan... I felt it needed to be known that this house was their home and that it's Alan's record collection. It felt important that they all felt present.

It felt important – as the whole play is a bit of a stretch: they are in their own little bubble. So if you are going to go along with me – if you are going to suspend your disbelief and accept that this is a plausible way to get out of the big problem... then I felt I had to give you, the audience, some concrete context that they actually existed in the real world.

NK: *Each scene or act is a different season – tell me about that and why you started with autumn.*

TW: Well, the autumn of their lives, I suppose – was a simple way to do it. And I basically wanted the seasons to mirror the action... to get colder... and then warmer for summer. Once I'd decided that, I had to follow it through. I wanted it to be a whole year and I wanted to have the opportunity to time-jump neatly when it was needed for dramatic purposes, to show their decline but I didn't want it to happen over several years as there was no way they wouldn't be found over that length of time so a year was about the stretch we could have, and in a 45 to 50 minute play it felt about right. But then again I'm saying all this – but at the time I had two weeks to write it and I thought four scenes would be an easy way to divide it up, four quarters, and then it came out as it came out. I think that's the practical answer.

The seasons were very useful to root us in reality. And it was convenient. It allowed me to write the big speech about walking into snow, for example.

And weather is so important to rural communities.

And you needed the cold – if it wasn't cold they wouldn't have needed fuels. The weather needed to be a threat.

NK: *Did you do any research for this and if so, what research did you do?*

TW: I did no research at all. I did absolutely no research for this. It all happened so quickly. And it was a comedy. Once you've got two characters on an exercise bike, hooked up to a turbine, the audience isn't too bothered about whether you have researched it or not; and that's the great thing about writing plays rather than say novels – you don't have to describe anything. You just write the stage direction and that's for someone else to deal with.

Oh. Well there was the emotional research.

And it's a proto-disability play: its about independence.

I didn't really know that at the time but I was writing about my own independence, really… so I feel I had done years of emotional research – and the listening to what mattered to my grandparents too.

NK: *What do you hope for in future productions of* Windy Old Fossils?

TW: I would like the dialogue to be adhered to, or as close as people can. I have included the minimum of stage directions – things to help the emotional journey of the actors; but you have to make it work for your actors, your production, your space. The stage directions in the script act as a blue print but don't have to be adhered to. Finding that old exercise bike in a charity shop in Ludlow was certainly a stroke of luck.

NK: *Light and dark are big in the stage directions. Discuss!*

TW: Well, they are so connected: fossil fuels, light, energy.

I always loved the idea of starting the play in 'stage darkness' so the audience can see the characters but they can't see each other... that's immediately funny – them crawling, trying to find each other. That didn't change from the first draft. That's all I kept I think.

NK: *Had you seen anything that started in the dark?*

TW: I can't think of anything – but immediately there's a question – about what is going on. It's a good system for showing how desperate they are. And it felt real... we are always having power cuts in the countryside.

NK: *And the end. Did you know they were going to want to turn the light off?*

TW: Oh no... that came with the characters. Elderly people do like saving money. By the end they were more comfortable in the darkness… That was a nice journey – starting when they felt uncomfortable in the dark and ending feeling comfortable in it. That was a nice surprise.

NK: *Five years on, looking back at* Windy Old Fossils *what are you most proud of? And anything you now feel you could have done better?*

TW: I think it contains all the bits I like about my style… it's very much me. I suppose now I am more used to companies putting more of their stamp on the work, and so this is the closest to my speaking voice that I've written as a playwright.

I am really proud of it. It hit the target for the festival; people have remembered it and enjoyed it. I wouldn't rewrite it just because my writing has improved.

I like the characters and situation. The situation is still prevalent. We are still not seeing enough older actors and their stories. And it was the first Pentabus festival and their young writers' group is still continuing and now it has spawned this new Young Company – I am so very proud to have been part of the first eight.

NK: *What advice would you give to a new or emerging playwright?*

TW: Finish the play.
And then you will know what you've got.
Then, at least, you will have the first draft.

I mean if I had never finished the first *Windy* draft I would never have got to the Ted and Lizzie story.

REVIEWS OF *BURKE AND HARE*

Written by: Tom Wentworth

A Watermill Theatre production, Spring 2018
that transferred to London's Jermyn Street Theatre
for their Pre-Xmas run 2018
Originally created by Jenny Wren Productions

Directed by: Abigail Pickard Price
Starring: Katy Daghorn, Alex Parry and Hayden Wood

Pitch-black and wickedly funny… Tom Wentworth's
writing pitches the title characters' nefarious deeds as
a thrilling yarn rather than a cautionary tale. Quickfire
changes, asides to the audience and rousing musical
interludes lend the show a vaudevillian flavour and
Abigail Pickard Price's precise direction has clearly
paid off: slick slapstick timing ensures the pace
continues at a lick.

The Stage

Written by Tom Wentworth and performed
by a nimble cast of three, it's a gleeful mash-up
of history and prurient penny-dreadful scandal,
fast, funny and ever so slightly sick.

The Sunday Times

An absolute blast…rapid, adept and funny.
Libby Purves

Hare raising hilarity…drop dead funny
Reviews Gate

An instantly likeable, rip-roaring treatment of an old
tale makes this production irresistible.
Everything Theatre

I loved every black comedy minute of it, laughing
with tears streaming down my face.
Remote Goat

Thoroughly recommended
as an uproarious evening out!
London Theatre 1

The raucous script
and the company's comedic chemistry… own the
tongue-in-cheek jet-black humour and deploy
weapons of mass-hilarity.
Broadway World